A **NOVA** BOOK

Garbage!

Where It Comes From, Where It Goes

Evan & Janet Hadingham

Simon and Schuster Books for Young Readers
Published by Simon & Schuster Inc., New York

In association with WGBH Boston,
producers of NOVA for public television

SIMON AND SCHUSTER
BOOKS FOR YOUNG READERS
Simon & Schuster Building
Rockefeller Center
1230 Avenue of the Americas
New York, New York 10020

SIMON AND SCHUSTER
BOOKS FOR YOUNG READERS
is a trademark of
Simon & Schuster Inc.

Manufactured in the United States
of America.

10 9 8 7 6 5 4 3 2 1
10 9 8 7 6 5 4 3 2 1 (pbk.)
Library of Congress
Cataloging-in-Publication Data
   Garbage!: where it comes from,
where it goes/ Evan Hadingham & Janet
Hadingham.
   (A NOVABOOK)
   "In association with WGBH Boston,
producers of NOVA for public televi-
sion."
   Includes Index.
   Summary: Documents the ever-
increasing problem of what can be done
to dispose of our garbage.
   1. Refuse and refuse disposal –
Juvenile literature. [1. Refuse and refuse
disposal.] I. Hadingham, Janet. II. WGBH
(Television station: Boston, Mass.). III.
NOVA (Television program). IV. Title. V.
Series.
TD792.H327 1990
363.72 8 – dc20
89-26205 CIP AC

ISBN 0-671-69424-3
ISBN 0-671-69426-X (pbk.)

We wish to thank the following
friends, colleagues, and experts
who helped improve the odor
of our text: Roz Grunman,
Don Hickman, Ruth Johnson,
Marcia Keller, Susan Schmidt,
Lawrence Millman, Lois
Packard, William Rathje, and
Mary T'Kash. The book owes
much to WGBH, Boston,
notably the book's editor
Karen Johnson, designer
Alison Kennedy, typographer
M J Walsh and design assistant
Nancy Goldberg. Additional
thanks to Virginia Jackson,
Nancy Lattanzio, Marianne
Neuman, and Christopher
Pullman, as well as NOVA's
executive producer Paula Apsell
and illustrator Elwood Smith for
his unique, high-spirited graphic
contributions. The idea for
"Amazing Garbage Facts" was
inspired by the book In One Day
by Tom Parker, published by
Houghton Mifflin, 1984, also
the source for a few of the
entries. Wherever possible,
garbage facts and figures
follow data given in Facing
America's Trash, US Congress,
Office of Technology Assess-
ment, October 1989.

The NOVA television series
is produced by WGBH Boston,
and is made possible by the
Johnson & Johnson Family
of Companies, Lockheed
Corporation, and public television viewers.

Cover: Cans for recycling at a Newark, New Jersey landfill. Right: More than three thousand tons (2,700 metric tons) of thrown-out computers pile up at the Katsu Ichikawa Company near Toyota City. The company removes old computers from businesses, **then strips them of electronic chips and other useful components. These are sold to companies that need spare parts to fix broken computers. Meanwhile, the leftovers are torn apart so that metal and plastic materials can be sold to dealers for reuse.**

Contents

The Land of Frozen Trash

Just over one thousand years ago, the Viking explorer Eric the Red landed on a windy, barren coastline that he called Greenland. He hoped the name would attract other Vikings to join him in what sounded like a green and pleasant land. In reality, Greenland is so far north that it is mostly covered with a thick ice cap all year round. Even along the coast, the soil is bare and frozen as hard as rock. You would think that few plants or animals could live in such a landscape.

Yet for thousands of years, small bands of the native people known as the Eskimo, or Inuit, have survived there by hunting seals, whales, and polar bears. Some of their villages are so remote that until one hundred years ago many of the Greenland Eskimo had never seen a sailing ship nor had any other contact with the outside world.

In the old days, there was no such thing as garbage for these hunters. In a situation where families often went hungry and sometimes even died from starvation, everything the sea provided was precious. Since no trees grow there, the scraps of driftwood that washed up on the shore were carefully saved to make tools, bowls, plates, and masks. And once a seal was speared, dragged home, and cooked, virtually nothing of the animal was thrown away.

Though the meat was the most vital item, the Eskimo found uses for all other parts of the seal, too. Its skin provided them with clothes and bags. Its fat was eaten like butter, burned in lamps, and rubbed into the skin as protection against the biting wind. Its long, twisting intestines were dried and stuffed with meat to make sausages. Its bones were carved into tools and toys. Even its whiskers were saved and used as toothpicks. And they never had to think about how to get rid of the few scraps left over. Once tossed out the door, every last bit was snapped up by half-starved dogs and foxes.

About a hundred years ago, the lives of the people slowly began to change. Ships found their way through the pack ice and brought cans of whale meat, tea, sugar, and beer. Families no longer starved and no longer needed to hoard every scrap of material.

Although life has become easier, many of the Eskimo's habits have stayed the same. Most villagers still throw the remains of meals out their doors and windows. The big difference is that dogs can't eat paper, plastic, and cans.

A village in eastern Greenland photographed in 1987. Today the eastern Greenlanders live year-round in modern houses.

An Eskimo hunter in eastern Greenland photographed in 1908. He steadies a bow drill with his teeth as he fixes his hunting gear. In the background is a summertime hut made of driftwood logs covered with sealskin. In the wintertime, several families shared large, solid houses built of earth and stone.

If you walk through a typical village in east Greenland today, perhaps the most impressive sight you'll see is the garbage mound. That's where the Eskimo toss old rubber boots and tires, pieces of wooden crates, and thousands of beer cans. All this garbage usually lies in a giant heap in the center of the village, sometimes piled up higher than the rooftops of the houses.

The people don't seem to mind living with their trash. In fact, they've never had to think of trash as something ugly or dangerous. Because it's so cold there, microbes and bacteria can't survive out of doors, so the garbage heaps don't smell or spread disease. In any case, there's little alternative to piling up the garbage, besides throwing it in the sea. It's nearly impossible to dig a hole or bury anything in the rock-hard ground.

Polar bear at the city dump in **Churchill, Manitoba,** in **Canada. Many animals have** grown to depend on garbage for survival.

In the far north, the cold, dry air prevents nearly all garbage from decaying. A candy wrapper dropped today will look much the same twenty years from now. Plastic bags snatched by high winds from rubbish dumps can be found hundreds of miles from the nearest houses.

Today, few spots are left anywhere in the world where you can't find a bottle top, an empty soda can, or some other kind of garbage. And even though most of us live very differently from the people of east Greenland, in some ways we're remarkably similar. Like them, our thinking hasn't changed much. Most of us still throw out our trash without stopping to think who will take care of it or where it will end up. The only difference is we don't usually see piles of thrown-out plastic, glass, paper, and metal outside our own front door.

Instead, our trash gets hauled away to dumps, or landfills, where it's covered with earth. And because we're running out of landfills, Americans now face a big garbage problem. While the total amount of trash we all throw out grows steadily each year, landfills are shutting down everywhere. In fact, during the next twenty years, over three-quarters of all the landfills in the United States will shut down. (Some will close simply because they're full, others because they're breaking health and safety regulations.) So by the year 2010, there won't be many places left for our trash to go. This book is about our garbage problem, and explores what we can do to help solve it.

No place on earth is too remote for garbage. American scientists have strewn trash all over a bay at McMurdo Sound, a research base in Antarctica. Because of the extreme cold, most of their junk will last forever.

The Stink of the City

Imagine walking in New York City on a hot summer day. Sweaty pedestrians packed on the pavements, taxi horns, police sirens, sticky air, and traffic fumes can all make your walk pretty unpleasant. But that's nothing compared to what it was like about a hundred years ago.

Back then, there were no regular city-wide collections of garbage. You tossed your trash in wooden barrels lined up on the pavement. In between the barrels were big piles of coal or wood ash on which you dumped the ashes from your fireplace each morning. And you probably didn't think twice about throwing food or even toilet waste directly into the gutter.

But when you ventured out for a walk, you could scarcely ignore the filthy streets of New York. If you were a woman, you were wearing long skirts and had to lift them frequently to avoid the messes on the sidewalk. On some street corners you could scarcely breathe because of the fumes from breweries, slaughterhouses, and factories, combined with the stink from the gutter.

Boxes, Boxes Everywhere

In just one day, Americans toss out 150,000 tons (136,000 metric tons) of packaging material. This amount would fill about 10,000 tractor trailers. If all the trucks were lined up end-to-end, they would stretch for 120 miles (190 km).

Wow!

AMAZING GARBAGE FACT

Putting out the garbage on Ludlow Street, New York City, in 1881. The sidewalks were littered with heaps of ashes emptied from fireplaces and furnaces.

Since 1900, New York's garbage trucks have improved, but the job they do has stayed much the same. At a city waterfront, trucks tip trash onto barges in 1980 (top) and around 1900 (bottom).

Get Nosey About Your Garbage

Be a garbage detective. Figure out what goes into your garbage pail: Is it mostly food scraps or packaging? Do some research. For one week, instead of tossing packaging material into your regular garbage pail, collect it in a separate cardboard box.

Then try to identify the different materials (plastic, paper, aluminum, etc.). Notice the many different types of plastic — some are stiff, others light and supple; can you tell why that particular type of plastic was chosen for each package?

Can you figure out the main purpose of each packaging item? Was it to keep the food fresh? To protect it from damage during shipping? Do you think any of the items are examples of *overpackaging* — packaging that's there simply to make the item bigger and more eye-catching?

Continue your detective work next time you're at the grocery store. Which are the most over-packaged brands? If you or your parents avoid buying them, you'll be helping to solve the garbage problem.

And even though today's car fumes can make New York unpleasant and unhealthy, "exhaust" from horses presented quite a problem in the days before the automobile. A century ago, Brooklyn's horses produced 200 tons (180 metric tons) of manure a day (enough to fill eight railroad freight cars). In springtime, farmers visited the city with wagons and removed some of the horse manure to spread on their fields as fertilizer. But by summer, much of it ended up ground into the mud in the city's unpaved back alleys.

Many of New York's poor neighborhoods were so filthy and overcrowded that serious diseases such as typhoid and cholera spread easily. One such outbreak in 1892 helped shake up citizens and officials, who finally realized that garbage had become a serious problem. But how could they solve it?

The first solution was to dump it at sea. Around 1900, most of New York's trash was loaded on barges, towed out of the harbor for about ten miles (16 km), then heaved into the Atlantic. Bathers at New Jersey's

crowded beaches were sometimes startled when they swam up against objects such as floating mattresses and dead dogs. In fact, the problem became so bad that New Jersey's state officials forced New York City to stop ocean dumping in 1933.

But even today, many east coast beaches are forced to close down for days or weeks during the summer. The reason? Washed-up trash, sewage, sometimes even waste from hospitals that may carry germs or viruses. Some of the garbage is spilled accidentally or blown from landfills close to the ocean, like New York's giant trash mound at Fresh Kills on Staten Island. But much of it is dumped illegally. While New York and other coastal cities were forced to give up ocean dumping long ago, the pollution continues. Some people with a garbage problem on their hands are still prepared to break the law and use the ocean as a dump.

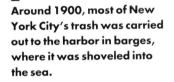

▲
Around 1900, most of New York City's trash was carried out to the harbor in barges, where it was shoveled into the sea.

▶
Trash dumped in New York's harbor would often drift down to New Jersey beaches to surprise bathers.

A Day in the Life of New York's Garbage

Every day, 1,000 garbage trucks crawl through the streets of New York City, each operated by a two-person crew. After picking up a full load, the crew drives its truck to one of thirteen different piers on the city's waterfront. There they put the truck into reverse and back it up to the edge of the pier, dumping their load into a barge waiting in the water below. Each barge can hold 6,000 tons of trash. Tugboats then pull the barges across the harbor to their destination: the world's largest dump, Fresh Kills, on Staten Island. ("Kills" comes from the original Dutch settlers' word

Today, New York's eight million residents throw out enough garbage every month to fill up the Empire State Building. After curbside collection, most of it ends up on barges that are towed past the skyscrapers of Manhattan and out into the harbor.

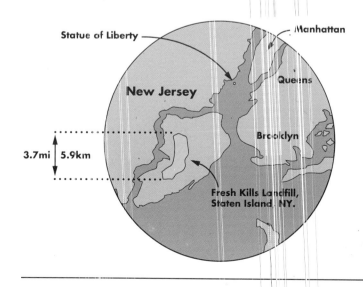

Statue of Liberty

Manhattan

New Jersey

Queens

Brooklyn

3.7mi | 5.9km

Fresh Kills Landfill, Staten Island, NY.

for "channel.") This dump covers an area of 3,000 acres (1,215 ha), equal to 16,000 baseball diamonds.

Once the barges arrive, giant cranes shift the trash into wagons, which are then pulled by tractors up onto the summit of Fresh Kills. Bulldozers help spread the trash and cover it with dirt. In summer, water containing insecticide is sprayed everywhere to keep down the clouds of dust and flies.

After ocean dumping was banned in 1933, New York's garbage had nowhere to go except to dumps like Fresh Kills and to a few *incinerators* (garbage-burning plants). For a while, dump sites were plentiful.

But as the city grew and more and more New Yorkers objected to living near the dumps, one by one they were shut down.

Fresh Kills is now one of only two dumps remaining in operation. The vast majority of the city's rubbish ends up here – some 22,000 tons (20,000 metric tons) of it a day. By the year 2000 or even earlier, Fresh Kills will be full and the city will have to come up with another garbage solution. By that time, the mound will be over five hundred feet (150 m) high – about the height of the Washington Monument. It will be the highest spot on the eastern seaboard south of Maine.

The barges finally arrive at Fresh Kills on Staten Island, where a giant crane unloads the trash and bulldozers push it around, creating a human-made mountain.

Every Day Americans Throw Out:

an average of about 4 pounds (1.8 kg) of garbage each. If you piled everyone's daily trash together in a single giant heap, it would weigh more than 438,000 tons (398,000 metric tons). Or if you managed to load it all into garbage trucks, you would need 63,000 of them. Lined up end to end, these 63,000 trucks would stretch for nearly 370 miles (600 km), about the distance from San Francisco to Los Angeles.

The Packaging Explosion

Back when your great-grandparents were children, a trip to a grocery store was very different from what it is today. There was much less packaging; and instead of picking up new bags from the store, you always took your own basket or canvas bag for carrying groceries home.

Many items were stored out of reach behind the counter. If you had a large family you probably bought big sacks of flour and sugar. (And when the cotton sacks were empty, you didn't throw them away. Instead, you bleached and sewed them into children's underwear.)

A few food items were sold in metal cans, but these were expensive. Besides, like most people, you probably did your own canning in glass jars that you used again year after year. If you did buy canned food, you kept the cans to store household objects like nails or buttons.

In 1879, a businessman named Frank Woolworth opened the first five-and-ten store in upstate New York. (It was called five-and-ten because back then many items cost a dime or less.) Woolworth was the first to pioneer the idea of displaying store goods on open shelves so that customers could see and touch the items themselves. This meant there had to be a lot more packaging of individual items, partly to catch the customer's eye and partly to make it a little harder for anyone to slip the items into a pocket and steal them from the store.

Packaging also keeps food fresh longer, and that helped to make the whole idea of convenience foods possible. But the popularity of items such as ready-made soups, cake mixes, and frozen dinners has led to an explosion in the amount of disposable plastic, paper, and aluminum we take into our homes at the end of every shopping trip.

PLASTIC-COATED SODA BOTTLES.

HEY, THAT'S MY TOY!

Today, in most countries outside the U.S.A. and Europe, there is little demand or need for food packaging. On market day at San Cristobal de Las Casas, Mexico, Maya Indians sell unwrapped fruit, beans, and potatoes on the street.

At the general store in Arkalon, Kansas, a century ago, flour, sugar, and crackers weren't individually packaged but were stored in barrels like those seen in front of the counter.

The food packaging explosion. Layers of plastic, cardboard, and aluminum surround the food we bring home from the store.

PLASTIC-WRAPPED VEGETABLES.

TRIPLE-WRAPPED INDIVIDUAL JUICE BOXES.

NON-BIODEGRADABLE POLYSTYRENE EGG CARTON.

EGGS

FRESH

NON-RECYCLABLE PLASTIC DETERGENT BOTTLE.

NEW LAUNDRY DETERGENT

FROZEN DINNER

FROZEN FOODS IN THROW-OUT DISHES

YOW!

ACTIVITY

In the Days Before Plastic

Ask the oldest person you know what it was like to go shopping when he or she was a child. Were there grocery carts? How many kinds of breakfast cereal were available? What came in cans? How were groceries brought home from the store? Was any packaging material saved and reused? What happened to food scraps? How was life different without the convenience foods we have today?

So many items crowd the supermarket shelves that food companies compete with each other to make their packages brighter, shinier, more appealing. That means a lot of overpackaging – far more than is necessary to keep food from spoiling. And it costs us all money: One out of every ten dollars you spend on groceries pays for the cost of packaging them.

Throwaway World

In 1955, *Life* magazine reported on a popular trend – "throwaway living." The 1950s were a boom time for middle-class Americans. They had been through years of restrictions and shortages during the Second World War, when they had to save every little scrap. Now they rushed out to buy disposable plates, knives, forks, frying pans, diapers – anything that promised to cut down on tedious chores. In this article, *Life* also reported on bizarre items such as disposable curtains, disposable duck-hunting decoys, and a 79-cent barbeque grill that you used once and tossed out.

While many items never caught on, a lot of products today are still designed to be used only once or twice. For instance, think of plastic shaving razors, mini-flashlights that you throw out once the bulb burns out, disposable cameras good for only one roll of film... all bound for the garbage, sooner rather than later.

Some brands of VCRs, hair dryers, telephones, and other appliances are built so cheaply that they only last a year or two. When they break, it often costs less to buy a new one than to have the old one repaired. And so it ends up in the trash, too.

What's in our trash:
This diagram gives a rough idea of the different percentages of materials typically thrown out by Americans.

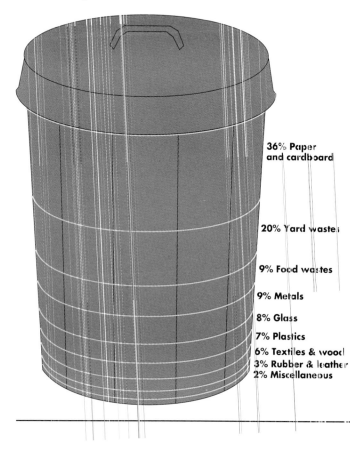

36% Paper and cardboard

20% Yard wastes

9% Food wastes

9% Metals

8% Glass

7% Plastics

6% Textiles & wood
3% Rubber & leather
2% Miscellaneous

Junk Mail Explosion

Do some research on your mail. Compare the amount of unrequested "junk" mail with the number of letters and business mail (bills, for example) that your family receives each day. Junk mail can include advertising fliers, coupons, catalogs, and requests for contributions.

In 1987, 10 billion mail-order catalogs alone were stuffed into Americans' mailboxes and piled on their front steps. This is twice as many as in 1980. Most of them end up in the trash – estimates of the weight of thrown-out catalogs range up to 2½ million tons (2.3 million metric tons). This is more than the weight of all the food cans we discard each year.

Throwaway living in the 1950s. Back then, dozens of disposable kitchen items like aluminum foil baking dishes, plastic knives and forks, and paper cups and plates suddenly became popular. *Life* magazine celebrated the popular "explosion" with this trick photo, published in 1955. The headline read: "Throwaway Living: Disposable Items Cut Down Household Chores." In those days, few people worried about the explosion of garbage created by the throwaway items.

WOW!

AMAZING GARBAGE FACT

Throwaway Living in the 1990s

Each year, Americans get rid of 350 million disposable plastic cigarette lighters, 1 ½ billion ballpoint pens, and 2 billion plastic shaving razors.

Down in the Dumps

Though there's nowhere else on earth quite like New York's trash mountain at Fresh Kills, communities all over the United States have their own miniature version: the town dump (also called a landfill). That's where you (or the garbage haulers) take your bundled newspapers, bulging trash bags, that worn-out toaster or refrigerator, or those old tires from your backyard.

The landfill is really just a hole in the ground. Down at the bottom, your trash bag gets dumped in a heap with a lot of others. Bulldozers crawl around, push the bags into neat piles, then cover them with soil to help keep down the smells and the number of rats. What could be a simpler, more obvious way to deal with garbage? Unfortunately, there's a catch.

Back when your parents were young in the fifties and sixties, landfills were dug wherever cheap unwanted land was available – in old quarries, abandoned mines, gravel pits, and marshlands. Such locations were useless for building houses but convenient for hiding trash. Unfortunately, back then no one realized that dangers lay concealed in buried trash.

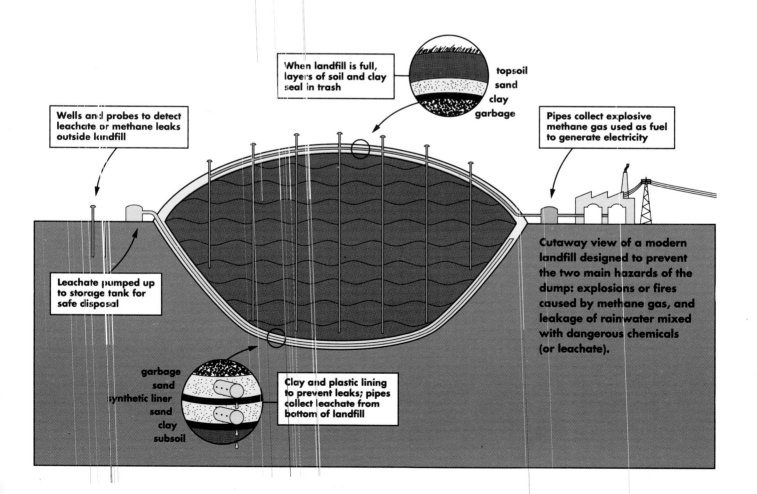

When landfill is full, layers of soil and clay seal in trash

topsoil
sand
clay
garbage

Wells and probes to detect leachate or methane leaks outside landfill

Pipes collect explosive methane gas used as fuel to generate electricity

Leachate pumped up to storage tank for safe disposal

Cutaway view of a modern landfill designed to prevent the two main hazards of the dump: explosions or fires caused by methane gas, and leakage of rainwater mixed with dangerous chemicals (or leachate).

garbage
sand
synthetic liner
sand
clay
subsoil

Clay and plastic lining to prevent leaks; pipes collect leachate from bottom of landfill

Landfill at Glendale, California. ◄

Plastic Is Forever

Why doesn't plastic decay like so many other materials that end up in the trash? The answer is that plastic is manufactured from long, complicated chains of atoms (molecules) called polymers. Bacteria and other tiny creatures find these polymers unappetizing; simpler materials such as wood and paper are easier for them to digest. That's why plastic lasts for so long.

Diaper Chain

Every day, people in the U.S.A. get rid of 48 million disposable diapers. Suppose you managed to unpeel the sticky tapes on each diaper and fasten them all together, side-by-side. You would be left holding a single messy diaper chain that would stretch halfway around the world at the equator.

Every day, products containing hazardous chemicals end up at the dump – products such as household cleaners, paints, oils, insect sprays, and fertilizer. Once these products are buried, rain water dripping through the garbage tends to break up the chemicals and mix them with the water. If this contaminated fluid (known as *leachate*) trickles down into a town's drinking supply, it can threaten the health of the community.

State and local officials now understand the risk posed by leachate and are enforcing strict rules and regulations to make landfills safe. But so many old landfills have a serious leachate problem that most of them fail to meet the new safety standards, and more and more are being permanently shut down. (In the next five years, 1,200 dump sites will close – one-fifth of the country's total.)

New landfills can be built that avoid most of the problems of the old. The sides of the hole can be coated with a material that doesn't allow the leachate to escape, creating a kind of leachate bathtub. The lining material is either clay, which repels water, or huge sheets of plastic. To stop the "bathtub" from overflow-

The Bottom Line on Diapers

During the first few years of life, a baby's diapers get changed at least seven thousand times. Most parents think it's an unpleasant job, and want to get rid of the dirty diapers as quickly as possible. So it's not surprising that disposable diapers are popular: eighteen billion are thrown out each year in the U.S.A. alone (that's more than three times the world's total population).

But like so many things we throw away, there's really no "away" when it comes to disposable diapers. When buried in a dump, the plastic material of the diapers will survive for centuries. And what's inside the diapers poses another problem. Though most manufacturers advise emptying the baby's waste into the toilet before disposing of the diapers, only a few parents bother to do this. As a result, it's dumped into public landfills – an estimated three million tons (2¾ metric tons) each year.

Scientists are still investigating whether this poses a health risk. Baby waste *can* contain dangerous viruses, including polio and hepatitis left over from vaccinations. Such viruses could pose a real threat to the health of garbage haulers. However, once the diapers are buried in a landfill, the viruses probably can't survive.

Perhaps the answer to the diaper problem is to design a better disposable. One idea is a two-piece diaper with a reusable cover on the outside, and inside, a thin liner that you could flush down the toilet along with the contents. Unfortunately, companies have been slow to market such a product, probably because you can make a much bigger profit from selling one-use disposables.

For now, the best alternative is to use washable cotton diapers. Baby waste from such diapers always ends up down the drain, where it can be channeled safely into the sewage system. The diapers themselves can be reused up to two hundred times and then recycled. And even if you use a diaper-cleaning service, it works out much cheaper than disposables.

A modern landfill in Pima County, Arizona. In the background, a newly dug hole is ready to be filled with trash. Huge sheets of plastic are stretched over the hole's sides to collect leachate.

ing, drainpipes are installed at the bottom of the hole so the leachate can be pumped out.

But like most answers to garbage problems, this one isn't perfect. The poisonous leachate that's pumped out still has to be dumped somewhere – usually in another landfill! The new landfills are also expensive to build and operate, and after a few years even plastic liners will start to leak. Anyway, nobody likes the idea of a landfill, old or new, in their neighborhood. The result? New landfills are scarce and getting scarcer. In fact, old ones are closing down more than twice as fast as new ones are opening up.

A Rotten Story

So what really happens to garbage? If you keep a trash bag hanging around your kitchen too long in the summer, you'll know. Those smells are due to the rotting of food scraps, and they're caused by the activities of millions of microscopic organisms – mostly fungi and bacteria. They live by digesting the complex natural chemicals that are found in all foods. They break these chemicals down into much simpler substances, and as they do so, they give off smelly gases (such as methane and hydrogen sulphide). They're also often helped by bigger creatures such as insects, worms, and mites.

Dig a Garbage Graveyard

Try an experiment in your backyard. Bury some food scraps side-by-side with other materials such as paper, plastic, and aluminum. Then dig them up a month later. Which materials are beginning to break down and rot (or biodegrade)? Which aren't?

The Natural "Garbage" Cycle
All living things depend on nature's nutrient cycle

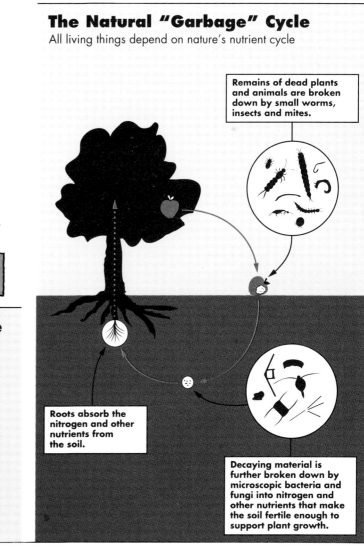

Remains of dead plants and animals are broken down by small worms, insects and mites.

Roots absorb the nitrogen and other nutrients from the soil.

Decaying material is further broken down by microscopic bacteria and fungi into nitrogen and other nutrients that make the soil fertile enough to support plant growth.

The Case of the Vanishing Trash Bag

A lot of people are concerned not only about trash itself, but also about what we put it into – the (usually plastic) trash bag. In many stores you can now buy trash bags made from so-called "biodegradable" plastic. "Biodegradable" makes it sound as if this special plastic will decompose and eventually just disappear. But will it?

The special bags are made in two ways. The first way is to mix ordinary plastic with a biodegradable material like cornstarch. Bacteria can't eat plastic but they *will* eat cornstarch, so they attack the bag. The tiny organisms cause it to decompose, leaving behind tiny shreds of plastic. At least, that's what's supposed to happen. In fact, most of these trash bags will end up in a landfill where *nothing* breaks down easily, no matter how biodegradable it is.

The second way is to mix ordinary plastic with a chemical that decomposes when it's exposed to strong light. Since the plastic will only disintegrate if it's left out in the sun, this type seems to be designed for litterbugs, not landfills.

The manufacturers claim that both types of plastic will keep on breaking down into smaller and smaller pieces until they disappear. But since nobody tested these bags before they were marketed, there are a lot of unanswered questions. Will the plastic fragments totally vanish? How long will it take? Will the plastic leave some remnants that could be harmful?

In 1988, Gene Handlan, who runs a recycling program in Lincoln, Nebraska, decided to test the bags for himself. After burying them in a compost heap for two months, he found that although part of the plastic (25-60 percent) *had* disappeared, the remaining part failed to break down. He also found small amounts of lead chromate in the compost. This harmful chemical came from the yellow dye used to color the bags.

By using the word "biodegradable," manufacturers give people the wrong idea that the new bags will vanish after they're thrown away. This misleading idea will probably only make the garbage problem worse. Many people will assume there's no need to worry about throwing out this kind of plastic waste. And if people believe that plastic trash will disappear, they may even think it's OK to litter.

The whole idea of "biodegradable" plastics is not only misleading; it could also draw attention away from more promising answers to the waste problem. These include reducing the amount of plastic we use and developing new methods to recycle the plastic we throw away.

While our noses don't appreciate this activity, life on earth wouldn't be possible without it. All living plants need the simple substances (such as nitrogen) left over after the bacteria and fungi have done their work. Without them, our soils would quickly become exhausted and sterile, and most plant growth would grind to a halt. And pretty soon we would be surrounded by garbage of all kinds – including vast piles of perfectly preserved dead leaves, trees, bushes, and grasses – that would never rot.

Fortunately, fungi and bacteria find the remains of most dead plants and animals easy to break down. We use the word *biodegradable* to refer to substances that decompose quickly, such as dead leaves. A lot of

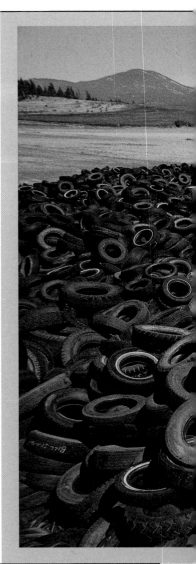

Garbage piling up at the edge of marshlands at Boxboro, Massachusetts. Old landfills were often located with little thought for the environment. However, we now know that chemicals leaking from such dumps can endanger wildlife and public water supplies.

human-made materials such as plastic aren't biodegradable – they break down very slowly, if at all.

Many people assume that we can help solve the garbage problem by shopping only for biodegradable products and packaging, and by avoiding plastic wrappers and containers. But the problem isn't that simple. Bacteria need more than just a good supply of biodegradable material; they also need plenty of oxygen from either the surrounding air or water. Deep inside most landfills, way down under tons of squashed trash, there's usually not nearly enough air or water for bacteria to thrive.

What's the result? In many landfills, garbage layers near the surface will rot, but most of the trash down below stays intact – whether it's biodegradable or not.

For instance, waste paper, which many people think of as a "natural," biodegradable material, can last almost forever if the trash layers are dry and squashed enough. In fact, paper is the single biggest item in most landfills, taking up far more space than any other material, including plastic.

The lesson is that if we want to try and solve the garbage problem, we have to cut down on *all* kinds of things we throw away, not just the ones we think will last longer.

Tire Trash Trouble

Car and truck owners in the U.S.A. throw out 200 million tires each year. If that number of tires were laid out in a single line, they would stretch for about 140,000 miles (180,000 km) . . . nearly 4½ times around the world at the equator.

When thrown-out car and truck tires arrive at the dump, they can pose serious hazards. They provide excellent breeding places for rats and mosquitoes, while they can easily smolder or burst into flames during hot weather.

Though about 15 million old tires are recycled and turned into "new" ones again each year, the number of recycled tires is actually going down each year. The market is shrinking because of the popularity of new blends of rubber and steel-belted tires, neither of which can be made easily from old tires.

◄
**Tire dump near
Davenport, Washington.**

Dangers from the Dumps

Garbage can explode. You don't need to throw out dangerous chemicals to make garbage explode – ordinary food scraps will do the job. Luckily, it doesn't happen in your kitchen garbage pail, but only when large amounts of household trash are buried in a landfill under just the right conditions. If bacteria digest the trash fast enough, they produce a special blend of gases – mostly carbon dioxide and methane. And if the methane gets trapped underground inside the landfill, it can explode.

Fortunately, few houses are situated close to landfills, so there's little risk of damage or injury from a methane explosion. In fact, if landfills are properly managed, explosions can be avoided, and the methane can provide a useful source of energy. Long before it builds up to a dangerous pressure, the gas is collected through a system of pipes. Usually, the pipes feed it into a furnace, which heats up a steam generator and produces electricity. Sometimes, instead of producing electricity, the gas is specially cleaned and processed so that it's suitable for fueling household cooking stoves.

Only about 120 methane recovery plants now operate in the United States, but they are a surprisingly effective source of power. A single large landfill can meet the energy needs of 10,000 families. We can get energy back from what we throw away – what we toss in our kitchen garbage pails can come back to cook another meal!

TV Toss-Out

Americans throw out their old televisions at an amazing rate: about 20,000 end up in the garbage every day. If you stacked them on top of each other, they would reach almost as high as Mt. Everest.

Garbage makes gas. At a landfill in Johnston, Rhode Island, methane gas, generated by the digestive process of bacteria eating deep within the layers of trash, is burned off to avoid the risk of uncontrolled fires or explosions.

So Where Will All Our Garbage Go?

Some communities have grown so desperate that they are actually shipping their trash hundreds of miles in search of a dump site. For instance, in 1986, New York State officials closed down an unsafe landfill in the town of Oyster Bay, Long Island, so there was nowhere for the town's trash to go. To reach the nearest open landfill in Taylor, Pennsylvania, 160 miles (260 km) away, truck drivers had to spend six hours a day driving Oyster Bay's trash on interstate highways. But that was just the beginning.

Later that year, the Taylor site was declared unsafe by Pennsylvania officials and closed. The same thing happened at the next Pennsylvania landfill. There the officials fined greedy dump operators half a million dollars for trying to stuff nearly six times the permitted daily amount of trash into their landfill.

When this second dump closed in May 1987, Oyster Bay truckers were forced to look farther west. The only landfills that would accept their garbage were now situated almost halfway across the country. Marathon trips began to sites in Michigan (over six hundred miles away) and Kentucky (over eight hundred miles away). Meanwhile, people living on Long Island had to pay huge taxes to cover the cost of these incredible trash trips.

Trucking garbage around the country doesn't really solve anything. It just means the landfills that *are* still open will fill up even faster. Meanwhile, some Americans' trash is sent on even more bizarre adventures – right out of the country and onto the high seas.

Garbaeology

Archaeologists love garbage. They discover clues about ancient people in the remnants of meals and tools thrown out and buried long ago at prehistoric dwelling sites. But University of Arizona archaeologist Bill Rathje is interested in more recent sites – the garbage heaps of the 1950s, '60s, and '70s. He's reached surprising conclusions about the landfills his team has carefully dug up, sifted through, and sorted.

Most materials buried deep in a landfill change very little. Rathje was surprised to find newspapers from the fifties that he could still read (see below). He also discovered that newspapers and paper packaging take up more space inside landfills than any other material. So using less paper and recycling the paper we throw away (see page 34) are two of the most effective ways of tackling the garbage problem.

A newspaper dated March 26, 1952, still readable after more than 30 years inside a landfill.

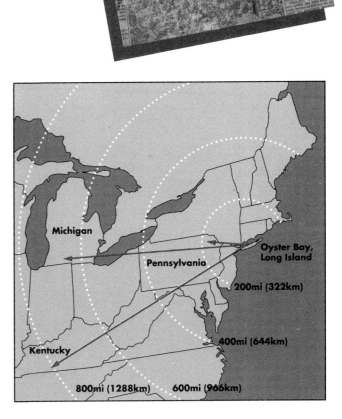

▶
Tractor trailers haul garbage from communities on Long Island, New York, to dumps located hundreds of miles away.

◀
But long-distance trucking of trash is becoming unwelcome in many communities where landfills are filling up fast.

Michigan
Pennsylvania
Oyster Bay, Long Island
Kentucky
200mi (322km)
400mi (644km)
600mi (966km)
800mi (1288km)

Garbage Pirates

A cargo ship owned by a Liberian company steams into the Delaware River after a long ocean voyage. During the 1½ years since the *Khian Sea* first left Philadelphia, the ship has visited the Caribbean, West Africa, and the west coast of South America. Along the way, the captain has applied for permission to unload his cargo at dozens of different ports.

But no country has allowed the ship to dock, for this is no ordinary cargo. The ship's hold contains 14,000 tons (13,000 metric tons) of concentrated garbage – poisonous ash left over from burning refuse at a Philadelphia incinerator.

Crazy Voyage of the *Khian Sea*

The story begins in 1986, when Philadelphia faces a tough problem: The landfills where trash has piled up year after year are now full. The city's garbage collectors can load the trash onto trucks, but where can they take it? Most landfills in neighboring towns are also full. Sometimes the trucks have to travel hundreds of miles to far-off states such as Ohio and Virginia to find a dumping place.

To help solve the problem, Philadelphia has built an incinerator, a giant furnace that sends most of the garbage up in smoke. But every kind of fire produces a little garbage of its own – the blackened ash that's left over after the fire is out. And getting rid of that ash from the incinerator presents the city with a new problem.

It costs so much money to haul the ash on trucks to a far-off landfill that a local company tries out a new idea: loading it onto a ship instead. So the *Khian Sea* sails out of Philadelphia, its cargo lockers full of ash,

In March 1988 shipping inspectors arrive alongside the *Khian Sea* as it lies at anchor in Delaware Bay. Its holds are filled with dangerous ash.

The *Khian Sea*'s cargo was toxic ash from a Philadelphia incinerator; this is a photo of the same kind of ash piled up beside the same plant.

and cruises from one country to another in search of a dumping place. International law forbids the sailors from simply throwing the ash into the sea. Instead, every time they land at a port, they offer large sums of money if local officials will agree to unload the ash from the ship and dump it somewhere on land. But because incinerator ash contains dangerous, poisonous substances, one country after another refuses.

After more than a year, the *Khian Sea* arrives at the island of Haiti and there, at last, some local soldiers are tempted by the money. Secretly, they help the sailors to dump about a quarter of the ash in a swampy area close to a beach. But the laws of Haiti forbid this kind of dumping. When the government hears what's going on, it orders the *Khian Sea* to remove the garbage and leave. The sailors clear up a little of the mess, but then, under cover of darkness, the ship slips away, possibly through the Panama Canal, leaving a small mountain of ash still piled up on the beach behind them.

Eventually, the Philadelphia company decides to give up on its garbage cruise: It's becoming too expensive to continue the search. Now the voyage comes full circle. The *Khian Sea* arrives back in Philadelphia, its hold still nearly as full as when it left a year and a half previously.

But this time even the city where the ash came from forbids the ship to land. Though the United States Coast Guard orders the ship to remain anchored in the Delaware River, the sailors decide to turn around and put to sea again.

Months pass, and after crossing both the Atlantic and the Mediterranean, a strange thing happens. In September 1988, the *Khian Sea* is spotted steaming down the Suez Canal, but it has a new owner and a new name, the *Felicia*. And there's no sign of the toxic ash. The new owner admits that his crew finally got rid of the ash somewhere, though he refuses to say where; most likely, it was dumped illegally in the ocean. So ends the ship's crazy two-year quest.

The *Khian Sea*'s crazy voyage as it searched over two years for a place to dump its 14,000 tons of dangerous incinerator ash.

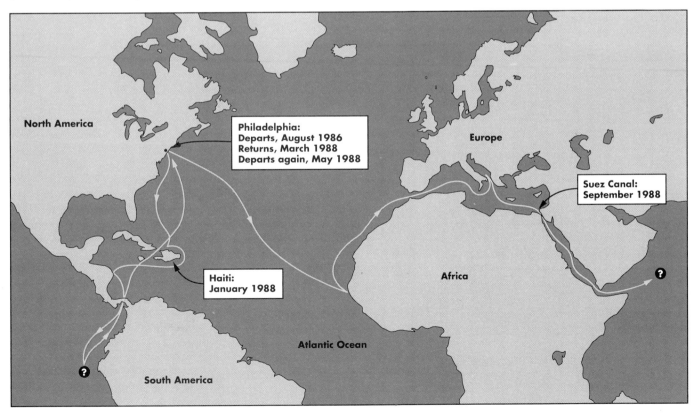

Dumping on Poor Countries

Though the story of the *Khian Sea* seems so bizarre, it is only one of more than a hundred incidents in which ships full of waste have steamed from one country to another over the past two years. In February 1988, for instance, more Philadelphia incinerator ash was shipped to the country of Guinea on the west coast of Africa. It was dumped illegally on an island, where it soon caused trees and animals to die. In another incident, this time on the Nigerian coast, leaking drums full of chemicals dumped by an Italian ship contaminated a large area of farmland. The chemicals caused sickness and injury among workers who had to handle the waste after Nigerian officials had ordered it to be loaded back on board the Italian ship.

Why is the shipping of waste continuing? Though sending dangerous waste on an ocean cruise sounds expensive, it's actually far cheaper than disposing of it properly in a special landfill in the U.S.A. – up to twenty-five times cheaper, in fact. That's why American disposal companies can make a big profit from shipping waste abroad. They can offer officials in African or Latin American countries huge sums to accept the cargo for dumping (in one case, $600 million). But such countries rarely have either the money or the technology to handle dangerous chemicals once they unload them.

Though the shipments may seem to solve a garbage problem for the U.S.A., spreading poisonous waste from rich nations to poor ones makes no sense at all in the long run. Since these nations are often struggling to meet their basic needs – food, clean water, health services, and education – adding dangerous chemicals to their list of problems is a very bad idea.

In fact, at least forty-five countries have banned the importing of garbage from other countries. And in March 1989, an international agreement was signed in Basel, Switzerland, in a further effort to stop the trade. Yet many people expect it to continue as long as large amounts of money can be made from shipping trash on the high seas.

Poo-Poo Train

In 1989, officials in Baltimore, Maryland, faced a problem disposing of human waste from the city's sewers. So they decided to ship the cargo by train to a treatment plant in Louisiana, over 1,000 miles (1,600 km) away. The waste was loaded on sixty-three open train cars and carried away. The only covering for each car was a sheet of plastic. The stench was so terrific that after the train had sat on a track in Schriever, Louisiana, for a week, it was run out of town by angry residents, who called it the "poo-poo choo-choo."

On the Hawaiian island of Laysan, an albatross sits behind plastic items collected by scientists from nests on the beach. The birds are attracted to the bright floating objects, then take them back to their nests to feed their young. Biologists on Laysan discovered that 90 percent of albatross chicks on the island had plastic in their digestive systems.

When Plastic Kills

When a U.S. biologist recently opened up the intestine of a dead sea turtle in Hawaii, he found it contained little but plastic – including a golf tee, shreds of bags, pieces of fishing line, a plastic flower, part of a bottle cap, and dozens of small chips of Styrofoam and hard plastic. The animal had slowly starved to death as its stomach filled with indigestible junk.

For centuries, sailors have grown accustomed to heaving garbage over the sides of their ships. Since most ports have such poor garbage disposal facilities, the sailors have little other choice. The world's fishermen currently dump around 175,000 tons (160,000 metric tons) of plastic into the oceans each year (that's about 2½ times the weight of the giant ocean liner the Queen Elizabeth II). While nobody knows the real animal death toll caused by this debris, some biologists think that as many as a million sea birds and one hundred thousand marine mammals die each year after eating plastic or becoming entangled in it – and that's in the northern Pacific alone. The mammals include seals, sea lions, dolphins, and endangered whales.

An equally big menace is posed by gigantic, nearly invisible plastic drift nets. Though these are illegal in U.S. coastal waters, about twelve hundred fishing boats from Japan, South Korea, and Taiwan use them for catching squid in the western Pacific. Each ship operates a single 30-mile- (48-km-) long net. The net hangs like a cur-tain near the surface and snags virtually any living creature in its path (including diving sea birds). When sections of the nets break or are dumped overboard, they carry on "fishing" until finally, months later, they wash ashore or sink from the weight of dead animals. At a meeting at the United Nations in 1989, delegates from many countries, including the U.S.A., called for a world-wide ban on this cruel and destructive method of fishing.

Besides international cooperation, the answer to the ocean plastics problem is to provide better disposal facilities in ports. In 1987, at the busy seacoast town of Newport on the Oregon coast, fishermen began bringing their garbage back to dry land. Under a program run by the U.S. National Marine Fisheries Service, the fishermen were encouraged to separate their trash into recyclable and non-recylable materials, and then deposit their trash bags in bright blue dumpsters at the dockside.

Since the organizers made a point of involving the fishermen and their families in the program right from the start, they managed to get enthusiastic cooperation. Some fishermen even made announcements on radio and TV, urging others to bring their trash back to port or to pick up any kind of floating debris. There were also parades around town with fishermen wearing cast-off nets and T-shirts with the program's motto:
DON'T TEACH YOUR TRASH TO SWIM!

Plastic threatens the lives of millions of marine animals, like this California sea lion trapped in a plastic fishing net, and this sea gull with its head caught in a plastic six-pack holder.

Too Hot to Handle?

If you had been living in Chicago in 1893, you might have woken up suddenly one morning to a startling sound. Down the alley behind your house came a clanking and roaring as a team of horses slowly pulled a giant oven on wheels through your neighborhood. Sweaty workers shoveled trash in one end while black smoke came out the other, billowing from the top of a white-hot smokestack. Every now and then, they paused to squirt crude oil into the oven to keep the flames going. As the oven trundled forward, a wagon followed behind in which they tossed all the things that wouldn't burn – ashes, bottles, and tin cans.

The inventors of the traveling trash oven thought they had the perfect answer to Chicago's garbage problem. For a cost of only $20 a day, they claimed, the burner could get rid of fifteen to twenty wagonloads of trash – sending it all up in smoke. They also argued that people wouldn't mind clouds of soot passing through their backyards for a few minutes. That would be better than living all year round next to a permanent incinerator (garbage-burning plant).

Chicago's traveling trash oven of 1893.

Modern incinerator in Brooklyn, New York.

But Chicagoans didn't go for that argument. They didn't see why they had to put up with *any* smoke while trash could simply be carted away to the nearest dump site. As long as landfills remained plentiful, the idea of burning trash never caught fire.

All that changed in the 1970s and 1980s, when landfills all over the U.S.A. began to shut down. Then burning trash started to look like a good idea again.

Burning gets rid of a huge volume of garbage – at least three-quarters of it goes up in smoke. (The left-over quarter is mostly ash, which still has to be dumped in a landfill.) The other advantage is that most new incinerators are designed to produce energy from the burning garbage. The flames heat up boilers full of water, which turns to steam. Then the steam is used either directly to heat buildings or to drive turbines that generate electricity. So there are two ways a plant operator can make money: first, by charging trash haulers every time they drop off a load of garbage; and second, by selling off this steam energy to local electrical or gas companies.

Though burning trash may sound like a good business, incinerators are vastly expensive to build. (New ones can cost over $200 million each.) Besides their high cost, incinerators pose a serious health risk,

Many people, like this Greenpeace protester, are concerned about the dangerous chemicals released by incinerators.

Fighting Back

In the early 1980s, officials in many cities looked to incinerators as a quick, easy answer to their garbage problems. They pressed ahead with dozens of new incinerator projects, often with little concern for the pollution caused by burning trash, including the release into the air of deadly chemicals known as dioxins. In some cases they chose the poorest sections of their cities as the site for such plants, not expecting the people there to make much fuss about the pollution. But in Los Angeles, the people fought back.

The story starts in 1983, when the city of Los Angeles began a project known as LANCER (Los Angeles City Energy Recovery Project). The plan was to build three incinerators, each designed to burn 1,600 tons (1,450 metric tons) of garbage a day and to generate electricity for 40,000 homes. But little attention was paid to the problem of pollutants. For example, the plan allowed for the release of up to 170 times more dioxin than is permitted at similar plants in Sweden.

LANCER's planners attempted to locate the plants in three Los Angeles neighborhoods where most people were poorer, more often without jobs, and less fluent in English than in other parts of the city.

For nearly a year they managed to keep details of the project quiet. In 1985, however, news of the planned incinerators began to reach the neighborhoods. Soon local people formed a group called Concerned

Citizens of South Central, which circulated information and held meetings about the plan. Their protests eventually led to new studies of LANCER that uncovered its many unsafe and undesirable features. Mayor Tom Bradley finally declared the project "a significant health risk," and canceled it in 1987. He also decided that the city should give recycling a chance to work rather than encourage any further new incinerator projects.

While many of the latest plants *are* carefully designed, including "scrubbing" equipment to prevent pollutants from escaping into the air, doubts remain about the long-term safety of these plants, particularly the biggest ones.

Another problem is that some incinerator projects are still going ahead – as LANCER did – without any effort to involve the community in a recycling plan first. As explained in the next chapter, recycling can't totally solve the garbage problem. But a successful scheme can cut the quantity of trash that a community generates by at least a third. Less garbage means lower disposal costs and less need for huge, potentially unsafe, incinerators.

As the LANCER story shows, some planners don't take the time to figure out a garbage disposal scheme that could benefit the whole community. The LANCER story also shows how ordinary people can work together to stop reckless "solutions" to the trash crisis that could be dangerous to their neighborhoods.

since the burning trash can send chemicals up the smokestack and release them into the air people breathe.

These chemicals include some of the deadliest poisons known. For instance, when some types of plastic packaging burn, they give off chemicals known as dioxins and furans. Even tiny traces of these substances have been shown to be terribly harmful to humans – for instance, they encourage the spread of cancer in the body, and affect the health of unborn babies in the womb.

Not surprisingly, fears about these air and ash problems have led many communities to fight against plans to build new incinerators in their neighborhoods.

Since 1986, such protests (as well as the huge cost of building plants) have led to the cancellation of over thirty new incinerator projects across the U.S.A.

In other countries, steps have been taken to reduce the pollution problem. At plants in Sweden, West Germany, and Japan, a new process known as *scrubbing* draws off the gases from the burning trash and "scrubs" them clean of many dangerous chemicals. That still leaves many of the chemicals behind in the leftover ash, but at least people in the neighborhood aren't breathing them. In Europe and Japan, the ash is sealed in barrels and buried in a special landfill under strict safety regulations.

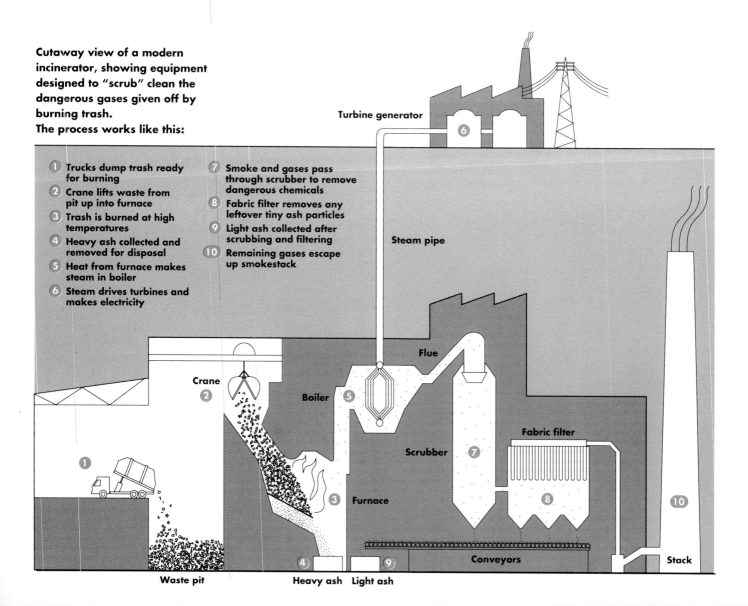

Cutaway view of a modern incinerator, showing equipment designed to "scrub" clean the dangerous gases given off by burning trash.
The process works like this:

1. Trucks dump trash ready for burning
2. Crane lifts waste from pit up into furnace
3. Trash is burned at high temperatures
4. Heavy ash collected and removed for disposal
5. Heat from furnace makes steam in boiler
6. Steam drives turbines and makes electricity
7. Smoke and gases pass through scrubber to remove dangerous chemicals
8. Fabric filter removes any leftover tiny ash particles
9. Light ash collected after scrubbing and filtering
10. Remaining gases escape up smokestack

Turbine generator

Steam pipe

Flue

Boiler

Crane

Scrubber

Fabric filter

Furnace

Conveyors

Stack

Waste pit

Heavy ash   Light ash

But as Americans have tried to copy the successful new European and Japanese incinerators, they have run into problems. First of all, the U.S. government hasn't yet come up with any rules for disposing of the dangerous ash. (In some states, you can drive it to any old dump site in an open truck if you want to.) Another problem is that about half of the new American plants have run into frequent breakdowns and repairs. (In fact, three such plants closed down permanently because they proved so troublesome to operate.)

The breakdowns happen because European-style plants were never designed to handle American-style garbage. Communities in Europe use far less plastic packaging than we do, and also recycle much more of their garbage. This means that items like glass jars, cans, cardboard, and newspapers are saved and reused, so they hardly ever end up in the incinerator. Without that mixture of metal, glass, and paper, the garbage burns more smoothly and breakdowns are rare.

These European plants have shown that incinerators *can* work and be part of a solution to the garbage problem. But so far, few American plants meet the high standards of Europe or Japan. For instance, many existing American incinerators give off chemicals like dioxins in quantities that would never be permitted in Sweden.

Also, most American incinerators have gone ahead without any serious efforts to encourage recycling in the community. Recycling not only helps incinerators to run more smoothly and with fewer breakdowns but also cuts down on the amount of garbage that needs to be burned. This allows smaller, safer, and cheaper incinerators to be built.

Batteries Not Included

Batteries – those little power packs that bring so many toys and radios to life – pose a special garbage problem. They contain dangerous metals such as mercury, cadmium, and lithium. Although each battery contains only a tiny amount of these metals, when you multiply that amount by the 2 billion batteries Americans buy each year, you are left with a serious problem.

When old batteries are thrown in the trash and get squashed in a landfill, the dangerous metals can leak out and trickle down into the local water supply. Or if they end up in an incinerator, the metal particles can be blown out of the smokestack and into the air we breathe. Either way, they risk damaging our health.

While the U.S. government has failed to introduce any special rules about the disposal of batteries, several community organizations have started their own voluntary drop-off programs. The programs involve dropping off your old, used-up batteries in collection boxes located at camera or toy stores.

The idea is simply to keep them out of your regular trash and so stop them from going to an incinerator or an ordinary landfill. Instead, they're taken to the special landfills in which other hazardous substances are carefully buried according to strict regulations.

Why haven't drop-off programs spread to every town? The programs would probably be more successful if people could make money by returning batteries. States would have to vote for a "battery bill" (similar to the bottle bills in force in many states, which make stores charge a 5-cent refundable deposit on cans and bottles). A 70-cent refund on batteries has met with great success in Denmark.

Meanwhile, battery makers have responded to the problem by reducing the amounts of dangerous metals, and by introducing rechargeable batteries. Although these are much more expensive than regular batteries, each one can be recharged up to a thousand times and can last ten years.

Battery Hazards: What You Can Do

You can start a battery collection program at your school. First, you need to contact your local waste disposal department and find out where they collect hazardous household waste. Next, you need to educate your classmates on the hazards of throwing out old batteries. Once you've got the support of your teachers and classmates, you can set up your collection box.

Recycling: The Many Lives of Garbage

Dig into history and you find that Americans have recycled for centuries. Two hundred years ago, women in New England villages used to meet at "quilting bees," where they would exchange news, gossip, and leftover scraps of cloth that they then stitched into new bedcovers and blankets. For many of America's early craftsmen, recycling was routine: Paul Revere, a hero of the American Revolution, was a silversmith, a trade that depended on melting down and reusing old silver.

Today, recycling can work out cheaper than either burning or trucking trash. The key point is to remove as much as possible of the reusable materials (paper and cardboard, glass, and cans, for instance), separating them from the rest of the community's trash. Of course, you can't reuse every item of garbage. You'll always end up with something to throw away. That "something" still has to be buried in a landfill or burned in an incinerator. But if the amount of leftover trash can be cut way down, it will be cheaper to get rid of it, and there will be less poisonous leachate or ash to worry about.

Loggers in Washington State chop down a 750-year-old tree. If the *New York Times* printed just one Sunday edition on recycled instead of new paper, 75,000 trees would be saved. But the *Times* is part owner of three paper mills that manufacture only new paper. Business interests and government regulations often make it easier for manufacturers to rely on new materials rather than recycled ones. The long-term effects of this are bad for our environment. Huge areas of ancient forests in the American Northwest are disappearing because of Americans' growing demand for new paper.

At a paper plant at Erving, Massachusetts, old newspapers are stacked in the background, ready for recycling. In front of them are piles of old rags that will be added to improve the new paper's texture.

Recycling also doesn't require the millions of dollars it takes to build an incinerator. The way the most successful programs work is simple. The town usually gives you free plastic containers, one for glass, one for cans, one for paper waste, and so on. Each week you set the containers out on the street alongside your regular trash bag. When the haulers arrive at your house, they dump the contents of each container into separate compartments in their special garbage truck. Then they take the truck back to a recycling center. Here the different materials are sorted, stockpiled, and eventually sold to mills and factories for reprocessing into new products.

In Japan, recycling has been practiced for hundreds of years. In public places such as city parks, you'll see separate containers for paper and cans. Recycling centers are more than just the temporary storage places they are in the U.S.A. In Japan, retired or disabled people work in these centers, repairing old furniture or household appliances and then selling them again. And in Machida City, not far from Tokyo, they have a program called *chirigami kokan* ("tissue-paper exchange") in which you receive free recycled paper products, such as tissue paper, napkins, and toilet paper, in exchange for your old newspapers.

Recycling human waste. Here sludge from a sewage plant is being sprayed on corn fields near Zurich, Switzerland. The sludge is an effective fertilizer, but it must first be carefully processed to remove harmful pollutants.

WOW!

AMAZING GARBAGE FACT

Tinsel Trash

Every year, 34 million Christmas trees are thrown out in the U.S.A. That's about the same number of trees as in a forest of 50,000 acres (20,000 ha) – an area roughly equal to 60,000 football fields.

While most American programs are still in their early days, a few have already proven as successful as anything in Japan. For instance, in only eight months, the city of Seattle managed to cut its trash volume by a third and to persuade over half its residents to sort their jars, cans, and newspapers each week. The program has been such a success that plans to build a new incinerator have been postponed.

Changing Our Trashy Habits

Despite the wave of successful new programs, recycling has its problems, particularly when it comes to materials like plastics. Only a tiny fraction – at most, 3 percent – of all plastic containers are recycled now. One problem is that old plastic can't be recycled if it contains dirt or contaminants like glue, paper labels, or bottle caps. Another problem is that not all plastics are alike: There are five different kinds of raw plastic material, called *resins*. Each type of resin gives the container a different amount of strength or flexibility.

To make new plastic products out of old ones, you have to sort out the different kinds of resins and then melt them down. The tricky part is recognizing the five different basic resins from a mixed-up pile of plastic containers. But new inventions – such as stamping each container with a special code – may help solve the problem.

New paper has been made from old for generations. In the photo above, taken around 1900, women in New York City sort through different grades of waste paper. An identical operation is seen below, at a modern Japanese paper recycling plant in the 1980s.

In the long run, though, it's people, not gadgets, that make recycling work. How do you make people care enough about the garbage problem to change the way they've been throwing things out for years and years?

You *can* persuade nearly everybody to recycle if it costs them more to throw things out the old-fashioned, wasteful way. For instance, in High Bridge, New Jersey, the town picks up trays full of jars, cans, and newspapers for free; but you have to buy a sticker for each regular trash bag you leave out at the curbside. If the garbage haulers see a bag without a sticker, they won't pick it up.

What's the result? If you put out a lot of bags, you have to buy a lot of stickers, so it costs you more to be wasteful. The easiest way to save on bags is to recycle. Taking the jars, cans, and newspapers out of your household trash saves a lot of room in the bag.

A *New York Times* reporter who visited High Bridge in 1988 found that families were changing their habits – leaving empty cans on the kitchen counter rather than tossing them in the pail . . . stomping on egg cartons, milk containers, and cereal boxes . . . even snipping up plastic bottles with scissors – all to make more room in the trash bag.

In High Bridge they even "recycle" vegetable scraps in the garden rather than dump them in the bag. The scraps end up in a compost heap in a corner of the yard, mixed in with dead leaves and grass clippings. The mixture soon rots and turns into useful fertilizer. This is the way just about all Americans dealt with food leftovers before the 1950s.

The lesson of High Bridge is that Americans *can* learn to be less wasteful, particularly if it saves them money. For instance, if you need to throw out a big item like an armchair or a sofa, you have to buy more stickers. (You have to stick two on an armchair, four on a sofa.) "We wanted to throw out an old sofa," explains a resident, Janet Nazif, "but they wanted four stickers on it. We didn't want to part with them, so we looked extra hard and found a school that wanted a used couch for a classroom."

Recycling Christmas

Look around your neighborhood a couple of weeks after Christmas. Abandoned Christmas trees lie on the sidewalk, scraps of tinsel clinging to the fir. But in Austin, Texas, there's a new Christmas custom. The city collects the trees and sends them through a machine that turns them into wood chips. They're spread on trails, under trees, and on flower beds in parks throughout the city. The chips help fertilize the soil and keep it moist. And they save $20,000 a year that would be spent on watering and fertilizing, and on getting rid of Christmas trees.

Making It Work

As Janet discovered, it often takes a special effort to find a new use for something you'd like to recycle instead of throw away. This turns out to be one of recycling's biggest problems. After all, persuading people to sort their trash isn't much use if you can't find a use, or market, for the cans, jars, and newspapers at the other end. Some curbside programs have been so successful that collection centers are sometimes flooded – the papers and cans pile up, and there's nowhere for them to go.

If too much scrap iron or waste paper comes on the market at the same time, the price of these materials goes down fast, and waste dealers can't make any money. With no money coming in, the recycling plan can fail.

The clear lesson is that many schemes can't make it on their own, at least at the beginning. Money from the state or local government is usually needed to support the program and keep the waste buyers in business when prices for recycled materials go down.

But even though nearly every state has agreed on the need for recycling, none has put much money into it. (In fact, so far states across the U.S.A. have spent forty times more on supporting incinerator projects than on helping to get recycling off the ground.) In many cities, it's enthusiastic, often unpaid, volunteers who are making the schemes work.

One of recycling's biggest success stories: aluminum cans. Making new cans from old ones is much cheaper than making them from scratch. That's why there's a strong, steady demand for recycled cans, unlike most other kinds of recycled garbage. In 1988, over half the cans sold in America were collected for reprocessing into new cans.

Nothing Was Wasted in Paris

A century ago, Americans were already throwing out more garbage than the people of many other nations. The writer of this passage from an old issue of *Scientific American* noted that the citizens of Paris, France carefully saved and reused items that Americans generally thought of as trash:

Even the smallest scrap of paper, that which every one throws away, here becomes a source of profit. Old provision tins, for instance, are full of money; the lead soldering is removed and melted down into cakes, while the tin goes to make children's toys. Old boots, however bad, always contain in the arch of the foot at least one sound piece that will serve again, and generally there are two or three others in the sole, the heel, and at the back. Scraps of paper go to the cardboard factory, orange peel to the marmalade maker, and so on. The ideas suggested are not always agreeable, and to see a rag picker fishing orange peel out of the basket is enough to make one forswear [give up] marmalade; but there is worse than that. The most valuable refuse – that which fetches two francs the kilo – is hair; the long goes to the hair dresser [for wigs], while the short is used, among other things, for clarifying oils.

Scientific American
September 1, 1894

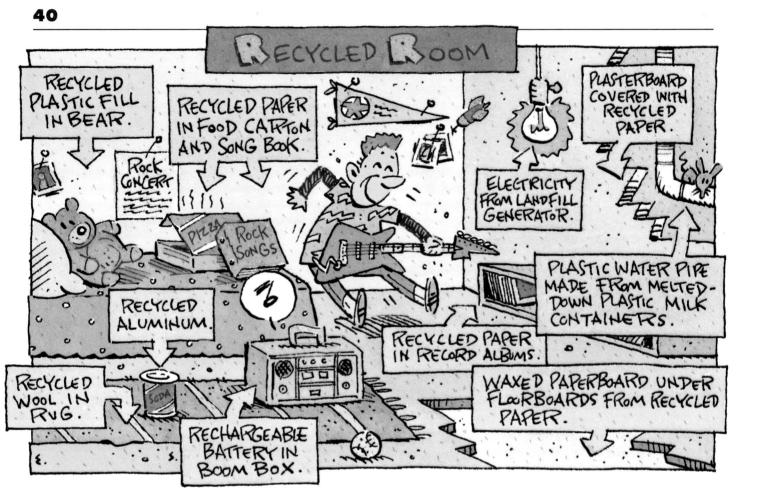

RECYCLED ROOM

RECYCLED PLASTIC FILL IN BEAR.

RECYCLED PAPER IN FOOD CARTON AND SONG BOOK.

PLASTERBOARD COVERED WITH RECYCLED PAPER.

ELECTRICITY FROM LANDFILL GENERATOR.

RECYCLED ALUMINUM.

PLASTIC WATER PIPE MADE FROM MELTED-DOWN PLASTIC MILK CONTAINERS.

RECYCLED PAPER IN RECORD ALBUMS.

RECYCLED WOOL IN RUG.

WAXED PAPERBOARD UNDER FLOORBOARDS FROM RECYCLED PAPER.

RECHARGEABLE BATTERY IN BOOM BOX.

Second Time Around

Even if you've never heard of recycling before, you're surrounded by materials that were once trash but were saved and used again.

Every time you pop open a soda can, for instance, there's more than a fifty-fifty chance the aluminum in the can has been used before. On the average, it takes about six weeks from the moment you take the old can back to a redemption center for it to reappear as a brand new can in a vending machine or on a drugstore counter. And recycled cans are much cheaper to make: making one from recycled aluminum takes only one-twentieth the amount of electricity that making one straight from the basic raw material, bauxite, does.

Paper cleansed of ink and returned to paper mills eventually shows up again in many surprising forms. It's all around you inside your house. It's in breakfast cereal cartons, game boards, pizza and shoe boxes, ticket stubs, book covers, newspapers, tissues, and toilet paper. If some of your rooms have plasterboard walls, they're covered with a layer of waste paper. Similar material is under the roof (tar paper) and under wooden floors (waxed paperboard). It's even in your family car – lots of it. As much as fifty to two hundred pounds (20 to 90 kg) finds its way into stiffening panels for car doors, seats, glove compartments, and sun visors.

All this adds up to a big demand for recycled paper. Nearly two hundred American paper mills now work entirely with recycled material, most of it newspaper and cardboard boxes collected from the street.

Though the market for recycled plastics is much smaller, it's growing steadily. About one out of every five plastic soda bottles is chopped up, melted down, and molded into new materials for making bathtubs, boat hulls, paint brushes, as well as stuffing for cushions, teddy bears, and the linings of jackets. Some plastic milk jugs are turned into plastic piping, the kind of piping that may carry drinking water to your kitchen.

Even the most unpleasant and apparently useless garbage of all – the stuff that comes out of our sewers and drainpipes – is becoming valuable. For instance, the city of Seattle used to dump all its sewage into the local bay. Now it is treated so that the solid leftovers (known as *sludge*) are free of poisonous substances. This sludge is then sold as fertilizer for fields, gardens, and forests. In fact, Seattle sludge makes trees grow twice as fast as normal, so local timber companies are lining up to buy the treated waste. At present, there's actually a local sludge shortage.

Protecting the Planet

If everyone in America recycled, and if there was plenty of money to support the programs, recycling still wouldn't totally solve the garbage problem. In fact, no single solution can.

Recycling can never be 100-percent effective. Even in a near-perfect recycling scheme, about a third of the garbage is left over, and this will always involve difficult decisions about dumping or burning it.

Yet in countries such as Japan, where both recycling and garbage disposal in general are more efficient than in the U.S.A., the lesson is clear. Giving top priority and support to recycling helps the other methods of disposal work more effectively. Japanese incinerators operate more cheaply and with less danger of pollution than most American ones, partly because the trash that is burned is so carefully separated and managed beforehand.

The lesson of recycling also shows that solving the garbage problem can start in our own homes. While it's easy to feel helpless in the face of so many worldwide problems, here is one where everyday actions can have a direct and practical impact. Every reader of this book can make a difference in contributing to a cleaner, less-polluted planet. The answer begins in our kitchens and at our curbsides.

Children hunting for garbage scraps at a giant dump in the Philippines in Southeast Asia. Some Philippine families survive by salvaging fragments of metal, plastic sheets, and other items, and then reselling them to waste dealers. This is an example of recycling, since thrown-out resources are being saved. But it involves a terrible cost for these children who must grow up in surroundings of dirt, disease, and poverty.

Does Your Soda Can Make a Difference?

So does the garbage problem really matter? What difference is it going to make if you throw that soda can into a garbage pail instead of taking it back to the store for recycling?

The answer is that your decision affects more than just your city's local trash disposal problem. In the long run, it could affect the future of the whole planet.

Today, the whole of the earth's environment is changing rapidly because of the soaring growth of human populations and industries. Our factories are using up enormous amounts of energy to make the products we all buy – and all too often throw away. The factories are burning off gases that pollute the air and that are slowly changing the earth's atmosphere and climate.

Air pollution – in particular, acid rain – is killing trees and poisoning lakes in many areas of Canada and Europe. The gases from factories are also contributing to the greenhouse effect, a gradual warming of the earth's atmosphere. Even if the atmosphere heats up by only a few degrees, it may be enough to melt large amounts of ice at the North and South Poles, raising the level of the oceans around the world and drowning many low-lying coastlines. A warmer climate may also have a devastating effect on farmers who even today struggle hard to survive in parched regions of Africa and Latin America.

Scientists disagree on just how serious the changes will be and how they'll affect our lives. But nearly all of them agree that saving energy will help slow down the greenhouse effect and make its impact less serious. Few dispute that saving energy should be a top priority for a prosperous nation like the United States.

Beer Cans at the Ball Park

In a single day of drinking, Americans throw out enough beer cans and beer bottles to fill a baseball stadium to a depth of 30 feet (9 m).

If you return that soda can, you're saving energy. (Making a can from recycled aluminum requires only one-twentieth the amount of electricity needed to make it from the raw material, bauxite.) In the same way, you save energy and trees when you buy recycled paper. (Saving trees is particularly important – trees help "soak up" the carbon dioxide that is contributing to the greenhouse effect.)

You save energy whenever you fix up and repair something instead of throwing it away and buying a new product. And you save energy when you pass on your old toys to younger kids instead of throwing them out.

Of course, recycling a can instead of trashing it saves only a tiny bit of energy. It's a tiny contribution toward helping out the earth. But there are over five billion of us on the planet. If everyone followed your example, the future would be brighter for all of us.

All you need is imagination to come up with new ways to reuse old garbage. This waterwheel made from milk cartons was entered in a river race in Seattle, Washington.

Facts on Fast-Food Foam

Fast-food packaging – those bright trays, cups, wrappers, and hamburger containers (or "clam shells") – is among the ugliest trash you see blowing around city streets. The use of polystyrene foam (or Styrofoam) for such packaging has aroused widespread concern, including attempts to ban it in more than fifteen states across the U.S.A.

Like most plastics, polystyrene isn't biodegradable; and if it ends up in rivers or oceans, it's particularly hazardous to wildlife. The foam breaks up easily into small floating chips that are swallowed by fish, turtles, and sea birds, and can block their digestive systems.

Besides its impact on animals, polystyrene poses a difficult disposal problem. Leading experts at the Society of Plastics Industries have judged it to be among the least recyclable of all plastics; there are only a few ways to reuse the old foam. And when polystyrene burns in an incinerator, it gives off a variety of hazardous chemicals. Unless the incinerator is highly efficient, those chemicals will reach the air we breathe.

The way polystyrene is manufactured raises even bigger problems than its disposal. To create its bubble-like texture, a special chemical has to be blown into the raw plastic material. Before 1989, the chemical most often used was one called CFC-12. This substance belongs to a family of other CFCs (or chlorofluorocarbons). CFCs caused worldwide alarm when it was discovered that they are eating away the earth's ozone layer, a thin protective screen in the upper atmosphere that helps shield all of us from the harmful ultraviolet rays of the sun. Increased exposure to these rays is expected to lead to more cases of skin cancer, among other effects.

Where is all this alarming CFC pollution coming from? Although polystyrene manufacture does contribute to the problem, the biggest use of CFCs is in the cooling systems of refrigerators and air conditioners. Whenever old refrigerators are reconditioned or broken apart in junkyards and landfills, CFCs escape and gradually make their way up through the atmoshpere to damage the ozone layer.

Yet since most of us visit fast-food restaurants far more often than we do junkyards or landfills, it's the foam packaging part of the CFC problem that has caused most concern. In response to public pressure, several fast-food chains have now switched from foam to paper packaging. And in late 1988, polystyrene manufacturers agreed to stop using CFC-12 for food packaging, in most cases switching to a less harmful substitute, HCFC-22.

This might be the end of the story, but foam packaging still causes a lot of public concern. First of all, HCFC-22 *does* attack ozone, though it is only 5 percent as destructive as CFC-12. Second, when HCFC-22 is burned, it gives off chlorinated carbons, which (like dioxins) are powerful and dangerous pollutants, even in tiny quantities.

Despite these problems, at least one major fast-food chain still uses foam packaging. In 1989, this company received permission from the Environmental Protection Agency (EPA) to build mini-incinerators behind three of its restaurants in Illinois, and was planning to build more in other states. These small furnaces are designed to burn packaging waste from each restaurant. Though the company is convinced that the furnaces will be safe, studies show that big-scale incinerators require skilled staff and constant monitoring to ensure they don't pollute the air. The operation of such furnaces by a restaurant chain sounds like a risky idea.

The same company has also supported an experimental foam recycling plant, and is encouraging customers at many of its restaurants to separate their foam trash so it can be collected for recycling. Since recycled foam isn't that useful, and making new foam from scratch is very cheap, this kind of recycling effort is unlikely to get off the ground.

While polystyrene has many drawbacks, so do some of the possible substitutes. Paper cups, for instance, have to be coated with plastic to hold hot liquids, and this plastic layer makes them no more likely to break down inside a landfill than polystyrene. A better idea for the school lunchroom is to give up the convenience of either throwaway paper or plastic foam and instead bring back old-fashioned solid plastic or metal trays and cups, which can be washed and reused many times over.

Kids Against Pollution

While we can all learn to save energy and be less wasteful in our everyday lives, that alone won't make the garbage problem disappear. We have to do more than simply pay attention to how we fill up our own trash cans.

After all, the big decisions of what to do with all our trash – whether to bury it, burn it, or reuse it – affect the lives and health of everybody around us. The decisions are influenced by officials in our towns and states, by lawmakers in Congress, by the heads of corporations, and by ordinary people who care about the environment. Our throwaway society won't change unless Americans everywhere – including children – get involved in those decisions. And as one group of New Jersey students discovered, children can have a surprisingly powerful voice in the decision-making process.

The story begins in September 1987, at Tenakill School in New Jersey, not far from New York City. Nick Byrne, an enthusiastic social studies teacher, was telling his fifth graders about the First Amendment.

This crucial part of the U.S. Constitution guarantees Americans' right to speak freely and seek justice for their grievances. If the First Amendment applies to everybody, the students asked, how could they – the kids of Tenakill School – make use of it?

Pick a topic, suggested Byrne, and then write letters to public officials and to editors of magazines and newspapers. Nick's students soon settled on the topic of pollution as one that affects everybody's lives and future. So they founded their own organization, Kids Against Pollution (KAP), complete with special stationery, a logo, and a motto: Save the Earth, Not Just For Us, But For Future Generations.

The original idea behind KAP was to start a network of information and action connecting several New Jersey school districts. To get the ball rolling, KAP members wrote to other students throughout the state and visited their schools. They didn't tell students what to think; instead, KAP provided information about many different environmental issues and urged them to write letters.

Field full of junked autos in Virginia.

May They Rust in Peace

Americans get rid of 20,000 cars and 4,000 trucks and buses every day. Lined up end to end, these abandoned vehicles would stretch for about 75 miles (120 km).

In April 1988, all the schools that had joined KAP sent their first mass mailing – 2,000 letters – addressed to Governor Mario Cuomo of New York and Senator Bill Bradley from New Jersey. The letters were about issues such as garbage on local beaches, recycling, sewage disposal, and acid rain. Soon the students organized a newsletter and spread their ideas farther by appearing at school boards, town councils, and even at New Jersey's state assembly.

One issue KAP members targeted was the use of trays and cups made from the plastic foam material known as polystyrene. Back in 1988, polystyrene was made with chemicals known as CFCs that are destroying the protective ozone layer high up in the earth's atmosphere (see box on page 44). KAP members believed that replacing plastic foam cups and trays with paper ones would not only help solve the garbage problem but help save the ozone layer, as well.

After KAP appeared before New Jersey school boards and town councils to explain their case against the foam, the material was banned from cafeterias in local schools and town offices. Eventually, under widespread public pressure from campaigns like KAP's, manufacturers started making food-packaging foam with less harmful chemicals.

Lessons from a Lunch Box

For thousands of years, people survived without aluminum foil, plastic wrap, or waxed paper to keep their food fresh. Next time you pack a lunch, think about the effect of each of these materials on the environment. What happens to either foil, plastic, or paper when you throw it out? (Is it degradable? Will it pollute the air if it's incinerated? Can it and will it be recycled?) What are the costs in resources when that material is manufactured? (For example, how much energy does it require? What raw resources – like trees – are used?) Do you have a reusable container that will do the job instead? Use your lunch box to set an example for other students who care about the environment.

Food Frenzy

In a single day, people in the U.S.A. throw out 43,000 tons (39,000 metric tons) of food. This is equal to the weight of about 50,000 compact cars.

▲
Members of *Kids Against Pollution* celebrate "Environmental Rights Day," a fund-raising festival they organized at Tenakill School, New Jersey, in May 1989.

In another campaign, KAP alerted its members to the hazards of helium balloons, which often end up in the sea and in the stomachs of dolphins, whales, and sea turtles. A New Jersey medical center agreed to stop launching its advertising balloons after it received letters from KAP.

KAP's work has shown how effective kids can be in changing decisions in their communities. The network has spread far beyond the Tenakill students' original expectations: Now their newsletter reaches over five hundred KAP groups in schools across forty-seven states. Members have addressed special sessions of the United Nations and the U.S. government's Environmental Protection Agency (EPA).

At an EPA hearing in 1989, one of KAP's founders, Cathy Bell, commented: "Sometimes we get so many letters requesting information that we just want to back out, get free of the responsibilities, and lead a nice, peaceful life again. But then we see some junk on the beach or trash by the road, and we realize that we really need to keep on doing what we are doing."

Help Keep the Lid on the Garbage Problem

Here are some ideas for things to do to help solve the garbage problem. Can you think of more to add to the list?

Save a tree

• Use less paper. Use both sides of a sheet of paper. Consider sharing a newspaper subscription with a neighbor.

• Take paper bags back to the store and reuse them. Better still, get a cloth or string bag and say "no" to paper and plastic.

• Use paper goods with the label Made From Recycled Paper. If more people buy recycled paper products, the market for recycled paper will grow.

• Recycle newspapers. If you don't have curbside collection, find out where the nearest recycling center is. Ask them what kinds of paper they take. (Some are fussy and don't want any colored ink or shiny paper – it's harder to recycle.) Write to your city officials and ask them to help make it easier for you to recycle.

Use less plastic

• Reuse plastic bags and packaging.

• Clean plastic picnic plates and cutlery and use them again. Most plastics don't decompose in landfills and if they're burned they pollute the air.

If you have a garden

• Make a compost pile with layers of grass trimmings, leaves, and vegetable and fruit scraps. Your local library may have books on gardening that contain hints on the best way to build your pile. (Yard waste and food take up over a quarter of the space inside most landfills.)

Get involved with pollution problems and recycling programs in your community

• "Kids Against Pollution" helps organize young people and inform them about local garbage problems. To find out about the nearest school with a KAP group or how to start your own, contact:

KIDS AGAINST POLLUTION
TENAKILL SCHOOL
275 HIGH STREET
CLOSTER, NEW JERSEY
07624

Index

Picture Credits

Cartoons Elwood Smith: 10, 15, 35, 38, 40, 44, 47, plus Amazing Garbage Fact and Activities icons.
Diagrams WGBH Design: Chris Pullman, Luis Alvarado, Julia Hänsel

Front cover Robert de Gast, Photo Researchers, Inc. **Back cover** Doug Wechsler **1** C. C. Lockwood **2-3** Matsuhiro Wada **4-5** Lawrence Millman **5** Johan Petersen, reproduced from *Angmagssalik* by N. O. Christensen and Hans Ebbesen, *Publikationer fra Arktisk Institut nr 1* **6** Dan Guravich **7** Keith-Nels Swenson, Greenpeace **8** Bettmann Archive **9** (top) John McGrail; (bottom) Bettmann Archive **11** (left) Documentary Media Resources; (right) Bettmann Archive **12-13** (all) John McGrail **14** (left) C. Allan Morgan; (right) Kansas State Historical Society **17** Peter Stackpole, Life Picture Service **19** Andrew Damon **20-21** C. Allan Morgan **22** Stephen G. Maka **23** Michael Mathers, Peter Arnold **24** John Nordell, J. B. Pictures **25** (left) Robert D. Hagan; (right) William Rathje **26** (left) Associated Press, courtesy of Greenpeace; (right) Townsend, Greenpeace **28** Frans Lanting **29** Frans Lanting **30** (top) Center for Environmental Education; (left) Documentary Media Resources; (right) John McGrail **31** John Smierciak, Picture Group **34** (right) Bryce Flynn, Picture Group; (left) Porterfield-Chickering, Photo Researchers, Inc. **36-37** Paolo Koch, Photo Researchers, Inc. **37** (top) Documentary Media Resources; (bottom) Bernard Pierre Wolfe, Photo Researchers, Inc. **38-39** Steve Elmore, Tom Stack Associates **41** M. Calderon, J. B. Pictures **42** F.B. Grunzweig, Photo Researchers, Inc. **43** Doug Wechsler **45** Lillian Bolstad, Peter Arnold **46** Nick Byrne, Kids Against Pollution